*Catherine Bramwell-Booth*

# *Catherine Bramwell-Booth*

## Catherine Swift

Marshall Pickering

Pickering and Inglis Marshall Morgan and Scott
34-42 Cleveland Street, London, W1P 5FB, U.K.

Copyright © 1989 Catherine M. Swift
First published in 1989 by Marshall Morgan and Scott
Publications Ltd.
Part of the Marshall Pickering Holdings Group

*British Library CIP Data*

Swift, Catherine M.
   Catherine Bramwell-Booth
   1. Great Britain, Salvation Army.
   Bramwell-Booth, Catherine, 1883 – 1987
I. Title II. Series
267'.15'0924

ISBN 0 551 01887 9

Text set in Times by Avocet Robinson, Buckingham.
Printed in Great Britain by Collins, Glasgow

# Contents

# Chapter 1

# *Christian Soldiers*

No matter to which social class they belonged, most Victorian children led rather unhappy lives. Many poor children were ill clothed, half starved and often homeless. From the age of four, many were forced to work for their living in the most horrendous conditions imaginable.

Mid-way through the 19th century, Acts of Parliament were passed to raise the age of child employment to nine years and to improve their working conditions. Sadly, those improvements were so slight as to be barely noticeable.

The rich child fared little better – but in an entirely different way. They had comfortable homes, ate well, didn't work for their living and were well dressed, but their upbringing was so strict that they were often whipped for the slightest misdemeanour and their expensive clothes were torture to wear.

Tiny babies were clothed in wool and heavy lace. And once they had learned to walk, children wore scaled-down versions of adult clothes in stiff brocades or heavy satins and velvets. Such apparel was so restricting to movement it made play impossible. Playing was discouraged anyway as the children were never allowed to run, be noisy, get dirty or untidy.

Education and religion were crammed into them. And teachers or governesses could be such tyrants that, simply for getting a sum wrong, a child could be whipped and deprived of food for the rest of the day.

Many times a day they recited long, boring prayers that held no meaning for young children and had very little to do with 'gentle Jesus'.

Sunday was a day they dreaded. All toys and hobbies were locked away and children were expected to sit quietly reading dull books. They attended church three times to pray and sing miserable, doleful hymns about the *love* of God. This was followed by a lengthy sermon promising the *wrath* of God and eternal punishment. So, apart from food and warmth, their lives were little happier than the poorer children.

On Friday, July 20th, 1883, in a middle-class area of London, Catherine Booth was born into one of the most deeply committed Christian families the world has ever known.

That may invite waves of sympathy for the wretched mite. What an awful existence she must have led, you will think. But oh, how different her life was from those you've just read about.

The Booths' home was filled with love, laughter, music, noisy, boisterous children and animals of all kinds.

Every day, in upper and middle-class Victorian households, the family and servants quietly gathered together in the sitting-room and, with downcast eyes and clasped hands, they listened while the master gave a Bible reading before saying prayers.

The Booths also upheld this tradition. But not for them a po-faced, unsmiling meeting with mournful music and meaningless prayers.

In their home, the older children marched round the room striking triangles, tambourines and banging drums. Adults bobbed the babies up and down on their laps. The servants clapped hands in time to the marching and everyone sang jolly songs about God's love; of all the wonders of His world and of what they must do to outsmart their arch enemy; the Devil.

Their entire lives were devoted to pleasing God, seeing Him as a benevolent grandfather beaming down on them from heaven – and probably tapping His foot in time to the music.

This modern attitude towards God had begun with Catherine's grandfather, William, son of Samuel and Mary Booth of Nottingham. Samuel was a builder of cheap property for housing the influx of labourers into the town at the time of England's Industrial Revolution. It was property destined to become slums before his children reached maturity.

While Samuel's business didn't bring him great wealth, he was comfortably off and able to provide a good education for this son, William. But, having more knowledge of bricks and mortar than of finance, Samuel couldn't sustain his standard of living and soon fell on hard times. And probably as a result of anxiety over his family's reduced status, he died young leaving Mary to bring up their son and two younger daughters. William was forced to leave school at fourteen and went to work as an assistant in a pawnbroker's shop where, continually, he was faced by misery and heartbreak.

The poor pledged their few precious possessions – a Sunday suit, a family heirloom, a wedding ring – for a few coppers to buy food for themselves or their children. Others pawned their belongings to buy alcohol. It was a means of escaping their misery for a brief time. Their intentions were to reclaim their belongings within days but often the pledged items couldn't be redeemed because, in their extreme poverty, they had no money with which to reclaim them. Then faces would be pressed up against the shop window, gazing at the property which was no longer theirs. Sometimes they watched more affluent people go into the shop and buy what had belonged to them only a matter of days earlier. This really brought heartbreak into the transaction.

9

While still in his teens William, following family tradition, became a Methodist lay preacher but by then he had already developed some ideas of his own about religion. Instead of seeing God as someone to be terrified of, he thought of Him as an endless fountain of love.

At the age of 20, he left the pawnbroking business and moved to London where he began to preach at outdoor meetings. Always he chose grimy street corners among the down-and-outs in the squalor of the East End – a place where God seemed unknown.

William gained some satisfaction from this work yet, although by then an ordained minister of the church, in his heart he felt he wasn't doing enough.

If people were starving, freezing cold and homeless, how could they be expected to attend church to thank God for His goodness? He realised that if the poverty stricken and the sick were helped with food, clothing, warmth and shelter they wouldn't need to be *told* of God's goodness. They would be experiencing it for themselves.

With these thoughts, William became increasingly discontented with Methodism.

When he was 26 he met the beautiful Catherine Mumford whose coachbuilder father, John, was deeply involved with the temperance movement; dissuading people from the evils of alcohol.

Even as a small child, Catherine had decided her future husband would be tall, lean and dark and that his name would be William. Also, he would be a sensitive man, a total abstainer from alcohol; more intelligent than herself, and a devout Christian as she believed she 'could be most useful to God as a minister's wife'.

Well, William Booth was tall, slim and darkly handsome. He was an abstainer, a Methodist minister and when he confided his new ideas on religion to her, Catherine understood and totally agreed with him. Yet, although he fulfilled all her childhood dreams, it was probably their kind, gentle natures which really drew them together and caused them to fall in love.

After their marriage in 1855, William relinquished his role as the Reverend Booth and left the Methodist Church to follow religion in the way they both felt was right. Catherine worked as hard as her husband but having had a sheltered upbringing, she was appalled at the sights, sounds and smells she encountered.

Starving people and orphaned children *lived* in the street, without shelter save for *newspaper* blankets at night. Besides filth and poverty, there was also terrible drunkenness and brutality. Drunken men beat their wives. Drunken mothers ill-treated their children. Starving children thieved for a livelihood.

Among all that anger, bitterness and crime, love seemed an unknown emotion but the Booths were determined to introduce it – particularly the love of God.

First they enrolled supporters from every walk of life; good people with others' welfare at heart. With their help, the new doctrine – The East London Christian Revival Association – was officially introduced to the world on July 2nd, 1865.

In the rough areas of London, they rented some buildings to use as kitchens where they made nourishing soup and bread. In small groups, others gathered on street corners, preaching the word of God. Those who stopped to listen were also told where they could get a good, hot meal for themselves and their children for just a few coppers or even free of charge if they were completely destitute.

As the news spread, queues of hungry, dejected people collected at the soup kitchens to be fed. Once fed, they were curious to know more about a place where, instead of being frowned upon or pushed aside like scraps of useless rubbish, they were treated kindly.

They began to think of what else they'd been told on the street corner; about the loving, caring God who only wanted them to take Him into their hearts. Many fed during the day returned at night to listen to the preachers, and a new world was opened up to them. In vast numbers they promised to mend their ways; giving up drink and crime to follow the Lord's teaching.

The 'missionaries' did everything to see that the penitents kept to their word. They visited their homes and families and, while continuing to feed and clothe them, they also sought and found employment for them. Yet these were people, some of whom had never in their lives considered working for an honest living.

The Booths were amazed at the success of the East London Christian Revival Association. However, some time later, William became disillusioned with both that title and the one by which it was more commonly known – The Christian Mission. This was after he'd heard it described as a 'voluntary' organisation. Neither the Booths nor their followers considered themselves *volunteers*. Some inner force was driving them on to save souls; to fight the devil and all he stood for. It was like serving in an army.

*An army*! That was precisely what they were – an army for God. One that would be trained to fight, not to destroy life but to save souls – a Salvation Army.

To fight battles and wage war on the foe, an army should be properly organised so, rather than have ordained ministers, *God's Army* would have soldiers and officers wearing uniforms.

Instead of a church, they would have a 'citadel' – a fortress which would prove impenetrable to their enemy, Satan. They would also need an arsenal well stocked with ammunition – rousing songs and military bands would 'fire' at the Devil and everything Godless. And that their battle cry would be 'Blood and Fire'.

There would be one noticeable difference from a military army though. In The Salvation Army, there would be children and women soldiers – and the women would hold equal rank with men.

Sadly, in Victorian Britain, many wealthy, respectable churchgoers thought this new outlook on religion vulgar and unseemly. It attracted common, low-class people; even criminals and drunkards. Surely the Lord would never accept them.

Brewers and public house landlords were incensed when 'Army' members became a threat to their livelihood by daring to preach against the evils of drink. They even rented an old pub, 'The Eastern Star', to turn into a shelter and soup kitchen.

Grocers were furious when The Army opened some shops selling meat, coffee and bread very cheaply to those who would otherwise have starved.

As for bands? The music they played and the songs they sang were all quite disrespectful and sounded much too jolly to have any connection with God and religion. But the worst thing by far was to see women in their midst marching along the streets singing and banging tambourines and timbrels.

So outraged were these *respectable* people that to show their protest, they hired known hooligans to start riots and attack the Salvationists. Some Army meetings were held in tents and it was quite common to have the guy ropes suddenly cut, allowing the heavy canvas to fall on the people praying inside. To enable them to see what was going on behind them, band leaders actually had to walk backwards because bands and marchers were often attacked. Street-corner preachers were usually pelted with stones. Many received serious injuries; some were killed. All sorts of ridiculous criminal charges were brought against them resulting in court appearances and heavy fines. In some instances, even prison sentences.

Still, The Army soldiered on.

# Chapter 2

# *Given Back to God*

When the Booths' marriage was blessed with children their lives were brimming with happiness. First came Bramwell, then Ballington followed by Catherine, Emma, Evangeline – called Eva – Herbert and Lucy. Sadly though, in the course of their duties, William and Catherine were forced to spend much time away from their home and family. William, now known as 'The General', continued the main work in London while Catherine worked in other parts of the country. Even this was criticised because at that time 'a woman's place was in the home'.

Eventually though, when they saw hardened drunkards and criminals reforming their ways, people started to recognise the good the Booths were doing.

In 1872, one of their workers emigrated to America and started a branch of The Salvation Army in Cleveland, Ohio, but before it became really established he returned home to England. However, in 1879, a family emigrated and settled in Philadelphia where they really put down Army roots, using an old furniture factory as their headquarters. From that small beginning, within a few years, The Salvation Army had expanded to become a world-wide organisation. Yet, although the Army's reputation had improved, in America some Salvationists were shot, stabbed or kicked to death. One man was stoned, hammered and jumped on until he died.

Nevertheless, wherever there was trouble; war, earthquakes, train crashes, flood, fire or famine, The Army men and women were usually first on the scene providing hot drinks, blankets, good cheer, comfort and prayers.

As the Booth children grew up their parents ensured they took on their own responsibilities within The Army. They also inherited the persecution. When Eva was only eighteen she was arrested by the police. Ballington was imprisoned for preaching in the streets and Catherine, who worked mostly in France, was imprisoned while on a visit to Switzerland. But it was Bramwell, the eldest son, who took on the most responsibility and by the age of sixteen he was a renowned preacher.

At twenty-six, he met Florence Soper whose father, Dr Soper, didn't really approve of the Booths' teachings although he was in favour of the good work they did. When his young daughter announced that she intended joining The Salvation Army he was most displeased, but didn't stand in her way. For quite a while she worked in France alongside young Catherine Booth who became her closest friend. This was how Florence came to meet Bramwell, and they fell in love almost at once.

When they married their homelife was on a parallel with that of Bramwell's parents. Florence adored her mother-in-law, and when their first child was born and the General remarked that the baby looked like his wife, they named her Catherine. But as his eldest daughter also bore that name, the General nicknamed his baby grand-daughter 'Catherine III' while his wife called her 'a dear little duck'.

As females had equal standing in The Army, it was assumed from birth that she would follow in William's and Bramwell's footsteps. But here the General saw an obstacle.

When Catherine III grew up and married, she would take her husband's name so he suggested that she be named Catherine Booth Booth. Thus, no matter what her married name was, the Army would always be led by someone named Booth.

Salvationists don't baptise their children, they dedicate them to God. And, being the granddaughter of the Army's founder, meant baby Catherine's dedication ceremony was of special importance. Consequently, a hall which held 4,000 people was hired for Monday, October 22nd, 1883 – the day when the newest addition to the Booth family would be formally presented and *given back to God*.

Of course, an announcement relating to the event appeared in the Army's own newspaper, the *War Cry*. But surprisingly, nearly all the nation's newspapers also carried lengthy reports on the forthcoming dedication and ran features about the Booth family and their good works. How times had changed from those first difficult days of the Christian Mission.

Services were held from the early morning but the baby's actual dedication was to take place in the afternoon. With heart beating furiously, Florence, who was only twenty-one, stepped forward to hand over her baby to the General. Lovingly William held his three-month-old granddaughter to his chest while she gazed about her, taking a wide-eyed interest in everything that was happening.

At moments during the lengthy formalities, as voices were raised in song and Hallelujahs, it seemed the huge building was in danger of losing its roof. Then Florence and Bramwell held their breath in case the tiny baby screamed in terror. But not Catherine. When the voices reached a crescendo, she merely looked about her with added interest then snuggled her head into the General's beard.

At last the ceremony was ending and William handed the baby back to his young daughter-in-law saying 'Take it, mother, take it. The father will help you to train it for God and The Salvation Army'.

17

Florence and Bramwell were the most loving of parents and each morning 'dear little duck' was lifted from her pink, draped cradle to be taken into their bed for kisses and cuddles.

Catherine was a happy child, always laughing and eager to learn. Sitting in her high-chair while her mother played the piano and sang rousing songs in honour of God, she would clap her podgy little hands and try to join in. One of the songs was 'My baby is a soldier and growing up for God'.

When Catherine was two, her sister, Mary, was born. Two years later baby Miriam arrived and, just like Catherine, they were both given Booth as a second name to carry on into married life.

At Miriam's dedication, Catherine, then four, was quite shocked. On arriving home she announced to the servants 'Mother gave the baby back to God. Right back to Him. But it's all right, she's bringing her home again in the perambulator'.

Two years after Miriam arrived came their first brother, Bernard. Until then there were no sons but that hadn't mattered one bit. Girls were just as capable of taking on the family responsibilities.

Very sweet natured, Florence had a unique way of acting upon her mother-in-law's advice to 'always insist on strict obedience'. If criminals or drunkards weren't to be blamed for their ways, then neither were the children. It was all the devil's fault.

One day when Catherine was naughty, Florence asked her to kneel beside her and apologise to God for upsetting Him. Knowing that wrongdoing didn't move their parents to anger but made them and God unhappy was more effective than any spankings or raised voices could have been.

Just like a military army, The Salvation Army has a set of rules called Articles of War. One rule is to care for animals. To oppose cruelty and never to inflict hard work upon an animal. The Booth household teemed with all kinds of pets: dogs, mice, rats, guinea pigs, a hedgehog and a pony and, because of their love for God's creatures, the entire family was vegetarian.

When Miriam was born, the young Catherine spent the day with her non-vegetarian grandparents. Seated round the luncheon table were aunts, uncles and some other visitors. As the General carved the meat her grandmother said, 'None for Catherine. Her parents don't give her meat so she mustn't eat it in this house.'

Everyone stared at the four year old who felt embarrassed at being singled out until her grandmother winked and gave her a big smile. This made her feel they shared a special secret and the awkward moment was gone.

In middle age, William was proving to be a hard taskmaster. Whatever he was unable to attend to himself, it was always a case of 'Leave it to Bramwell' or even 'Push it on to Bramwell'. He didn't stop to think how much responsibility he was piling on to his son, who had never known robust health and was slightly deaf.

Bramwell didn't mind the extra work even though it kept him from his wife and family. Every evening, he was expected to 'report' the day's events to his father and always came away burdened with even more problems.

Without a thought as to how it would be paid for, William would order the purchase of first one and then another building to create more places of shelter. Bramwell knew it was no use arguing with his father about the cost when his only concern was for saving people, body and soul. The order must be obeyed and with it came more worry for Bramwell who had to arrange yet another heavy mortgage. The Army was always short of money and charity was sought from everywhere to keep them going. As they provided more means of firing ammunition at Satan, donations were called 'cartridges'.

19

In February, 1888, when Catherine was seven, her grandmother, Catherine I, was discovered to be suffering from an incurable illness. And that day, after leaving her doctor's consulting-room, she climbed into a hansom for the drive home through the city streets. But neither the driver nor passers-by saw her drop to her knees on the cab floor and pray for help in telling her beloved William the awful truth. For a while, only Bramwell knew about his mother's illness because she wanted to spare the General's feelings for as long as possible. But eventually she could postpone it no longer, and one evening she told him that she had an apology to make to him. Thinking it must be some trivial thing she had overlooked, he was quite unprepared to hear her say that she was sorry she wouldn't be able to nurse him in his old age. This was followed by a painful explanation of the reason. William was devastated. Next, she told her family but on each public appearance after that, as she was seen to be growing more bowed and frail, the secret leaked out. Mrs Catherine Booth – The Army Mother as she was affectionately known – was very sick. People all over the world were dismayed.

To get her away from the city's grime and smoke, the General took his wife to live in Hadley Wood, near Hampstead. And because it was important that Bramwell saw his father every day, he moved his family to a house nearby.

The following April, when a great banquet was held to celebrate the General's sixtieth birthday, his wife was so weak she could only lie on a sofa in an anteroom until the meal was over. Only then did she manage to come into the main room for a few minutes.

July 15th, 1890, saw the twenty-fifth anniversary of The Salvation Army's foundation celebrated at the Crystal Palace in Sydenham, South London. Along with the entire Booth family, it was attended by some 50,000 people. But the joyous occasion was mingled with sadness for the Army Mother was too near death to be among them. However, part way through the ceremony, an enormous length of calico was unfurled across the stage. On it in huge lettering was a message from her which read:

I am dying under The Army flag.
It is yours to live and fight under.
God is my salvation and refuge in the storm.
I send you my love and my blessing.

When Catherine's end was near, typists were seated behind a screen in her bedroom to take down every word she uttered to hand on to both present and future cadets, soldiers, officers and most of all, converts.

Only days before she died her seven-year-old grand-daughter and namesake was taken to see her for the last time. As Florence lifted her up to kiss her, her grand-mother asked, 'Darling, do you know that I am going to heaven?'

This was the first real sadness little Catherine had experienced and it rendered her so heartbroken that she cried for ages. No matter how wonderful heaven may be, the young Catherine thought death was the most awful thing in the world and she hated the prospect evermore.

In 1890, twenty-five years on from the establishment of the East London Christian Revival Association and only twelve years after it becoming The Salvation Army, the founder's wife died – or, in Salvation Army terms, was 'Promoted to Glory'.

Crowds lined the route of her long funeral procession, which was accompanied by several brass bands. Mourning in Victorian times meant that even children wore deepest black – right down to the handkerchief. So how amazed people were to see the young girls in white dresses and all the other mourners wearing white shoulder sashes bearing a dark-red cross and crown. The Army didn't believe in wearing depressingly black clothes to publicly display sorrow. Grief was an emotion to be borne privately, in the heart.

# Chapter 3

# *Growing Up*

The following year another sister, Olive, was born. This helped to ease much of the sadness the family had suffered at Grandmother Booth's death. Two years after Olive came Dorothy – always known as Dora – and finally, after two more years, when Catherine was twelve, there came a second brother, William Wyecliffe, making seven children in all.

Florence had an office in London and also supervised The Nest: a home she had founded for abandoned and ill-treated children. She did other work as well but no matter what it was, until weaned, her youngest baby always went with her. If she was helping the family in a poor home where the mother was sick, Florence would place her baby in a basket on the floor while she cooked and washed for them.

Just like his own parents, Bramwell and his wife often went on long journeys together, attending to Army matters. They couldn't possibly afford the fares and accommodation for the children to go with them. And, in any case, young Catherine was always a bad traveller so, being the eldest, she took it upon herself to be the children's 'second' mother. She ensured that everyone helped around the house and, as her sisters and brothers adored her, whatever 'Cath says' was the law.

They were all educated at home, thanks to a great aunt who had bequeathed some money to be spent on them every year. With it, Florence had employed a governess.

And they were fortunate in having a French servant from whom they learned that language. Although Mary preferred the violin, they all learned to play the piano, guitars and cornet and took turns in playing for morning prayers at home.

It was no use Salvation Army children believing everyone was good, kind and well behaved or that, like themselves, everyone lived in comfortable homes surrounded by loving families. So, contrary to other Victorian parents, Bramwell and Florence never tried to shield them from the harsh facts of life. They knew all about dirt, starvation, drunks, criminals and down-and-outs, who lived in the streets and slept on the ground in *newspaper* bedding.

Florence was an unconventional lady for her time. Very concerned about diet, she insisted her household be fed on only wholemeal foods, fruit and vegetables. She didn't approve of patent medicines and avoided doctors whenever possible, preferring instead to use herbs, hot and cold water treatments, or other natural cures. She taught all the children to swim and urged them to walk barefoot in the house. She rode a bicycle and all the children received one on their tenth birthday – a day when, if it was one of the girls' birthdays, she was called 'the birthday queen'.

After his beloved Catherine had died, William had a small house built behind the one in which he lived. When he moved into it, once again Bramwell and Florence moved house to be near him. This time it was only across the way and into the Homestead, the house William had just vacated. It was a huge house with a large garden and many rooms, where the family could spread out.

Encouraged to play in the garden or the nearby woods and fields, the children would sometimes gallop along on imaginary steeds, urging their *mounts* to leap over ditches – an act at which they weren't always successful.

They sometimes returned covered in mud from head to foot and, being too dirty to enter the house, they undressed in the shed. On one occasion they were in such a state that Florence made them scrape the thickest grime from their clothes before accepting them for laundering. The children's high-spirited lifestyle wasn't at all what was expected of well-behaved Victorian children. In fact, neighbours called them 'the screaming Booths'.

Always there was love, love and more love between the parents and the seven brothers and sisters. They all called each other 'darling' and were never afraid to tell each other 'I love you'.

In the evenings they all gathered on little seats about their mother's chair for a story. And Florence made certain they were so positioned that by merely putting out her hand she could caress the head of each child while she read to them.

The children were all beautiful with golden-brown hair and hazel eyes, but, compared with their parents, they believed themselves to be quite plain.

Florence was very dainty with fair skin, bright golden hair and brilliant, sapphire-blue eyes.

The tall, dark-skinned Bramwell, with his black, luxuriant hair, side whiskers, moustache and beard was even more handsome than his father had been in his early years. But like young Catherine, he had ailed a lot throughout childhood and into adult life. At one spell, when suffering from a mild rash, someone advised him to shave off all his facial hair. When the children saw him they didn't recognise him and it was weeks before they stopped treating him like a stranger in the house.

When he wasn't attending to his father's or The Army's demands, Bramwell spent all his time with his wife and children. Blackberrying in the fields; picking damsons and apples from the trees; fishing; horse riding; going for country walks and creeping into Hadley woods behind the house at night to listen for nightingales and other nocturnal animal sounds.

Catherine thought her father was absolute perfection and even Florence expected the children to place him above all others.

In turn, Bramwell adored his own father and would always organise a grand welcome-home party for him after a tour. In 1903, after meeting President Theodore Roosevelt at the White House, William arrived home from America to find a bonfire party awaiting him.

By this time the once handsome General, who was a big man, had developed bushy eyebrows from under which sunken, penetrating eyes stared. He had a long, hooked nose, flowing, unruly white hair, and his beard, now also snow white, stretched down beyond his chest.

The young Booths were in awe of their grandfather's booming voice and his eyes that seemed to read their thoughts. Yet, when he was at home, Florence expected them to visit him every day. In order to both obey their mother *and* avoid the General they took it in turns which meant each one only needed to go once a week.

On one of Catherine's daily visits, when asked how well she had sung at the corps meeting, she replied, 'I did my best'.

'*You did your best*!' roared the General, glaring at her. 'Anyone can do their best. I expect *you* to do better than that.'

Actually William adored his grandchildren. Each Christmas he gave them wonderful parties and he loved to tease them, never dreaming they were a little afraid of him.

Whenever he was discussing world-wide Army matters with Bramwell, instead of sending the children from the room – as most adults would have done – William encouraged them to look up the places on the huge globe he kept on his study bookshelf. This exercise doubled

26

as a geography lesson and it gave them an indication of how widespread God's Army was.

By 1890, when Grandma Booth died, The Salvation Army was so well respected that every little thing concerning a Booth was reported in the newspapers. It was said they were like Britain's 'second' Royal family.

The public wanted to know what part of the country or the world General Booth, Florence or Bramwell were touring. They were interested in what the children did. If a Booth was ill, the entire nation was concerned. If the uniform was changed it was reported like a new fashion.

The General once said about music, 'Why should the Devil have all the best tunes?'. The same principle applies to personal appearance. Although vanity is taboo, the uniforms have always been very attractive. Over the years they have changed frequently, keeping up with current trends and avoiding a stuffy, old-fashioned image.

To begin with, women wore long, dark blue, full-skirted dresses with matching capes and poke bonnets.

Little girls' uniforms were dark stockings with dainty black, ankle-strap shoes; blue poke bonnets with ruched ribbon-edged brim and hat band; flared, dark blue, long-sleeved dresses, satin sashes, white collars and chest bands bearing in crimson the words, The Salvation Army.

On Sunday afternoons and evening The Army paraded the London pavements with long poles bearing collecting-bags which they held up to the top decks of buses as they stopped for passengers to board or alight.

Catherine, always a terribly shy child, showed no sign of growing out of her shyness. Constantly being mentioned in the newspapers really upset her and the prospect of preaching or collecting in public when grown up always played on her mind.

The idea of learning to walk backwards when leading a march or band terrified her in case spectators thought she looked foolish. But it was necessary to see if louts were following or harassing those at the rear.

She dreaded visitors coming to the house because the children were expected to leave the nursery or playroom and go to the drawing-room to be formally presented. Although the boys rebelled and kicked up a fuss about being 'shown off', the girls didn't mind; all except Catherine. She would cry and claim to feel ill. Still, Florence insisted they *all* make an appearance; always remembering what Catherine I had told her – 'They will appreciate your strictness when they grow up'.

From the earliest age, the Booth children were involved in Army matters. They began by preparing The Army's three periodicals for distribution and posting. Sitting at their huge dining-table, they folded copy after copy of the general magazine, *War Cry*; the women's magazine, *Deliverer*, and the children's magazine called the *Young Soldier*.

Each Sunday they either walked or cycled to the High Barnet Citadel, a short distance from their Hampstead home. There they would have religious quizzes and guessing games. Most of them played guitars and sang. As Catherine wasn't a good singer she played tenor horn or cornet instead. If the weather was fine the meetings were held outdoors and copies of the *War Cry* were sold to those who gathered to listen.

When she was only twelve, Catherine started helping to run a club called the Band of Love. As its members were all children around her own age her shyness didn't trouble her there, and also, because someone so young was in charge of the club, it put the members at ease.

In 1898, when she was fifteen, Catherine was sworn into The Salvation Army as a soldier. This was a very solemn occasion which involved signing the 'Articles of War' under the Army flag; a tricolour of red to signify the Blood of Jesus; yellow which symbolised the Fire of

The Holy Spirit, and blue to represent Purity.

Fifteen may seem young to take on such a commitment but in the year before Catherine's birth, when 700 Army members were attacked in the streets, twenty-five of them had been girls *under* the age of fifteen.

Catherine would have been content to hold the rank of soldier for the rest of her life, but she was *a Booth*. As her parents' eldest child, she knew that soon she would have to become a cadet facing a rigorous officer training period – and from then on, what and where to?

It wasn't merely her shyness and reluctance to stand out in public that made her want to stay in the lower ranks. Unlike the military army, in The Salvation Army it is only the officers who are stationed away from home. And once ordered to a post one is obliged to take it up even if it be on the far side of the world. Catherine was quite willing to accept orders and responsibility but she was desperately unhappy at the prospect of leaving home and her loved ones.

Her parents had never broached the subject of officer training and would never have forced their daughter into a way of life she didn't want. But Catherine wasn't their child. She was God's, for hadn't she been dedicated and been given back to Him. Wasn't she an instrument of God?

Oddly enough, at the very time leading up to her swearing in, Catherine began to have doubts, not over whether she belonged to God but questioning – *if there was a God*?

# Chapter 4

# *Doubts and Commitments*

Although, in her heart, unsure that she would have chosen to dedicate her life to God and The Salvation Army, Catherine felt she ought to honour her dedication for her parents' sake.

That word 'ought' seemed to haunt her young life.

Sometimes, on hearing of someone turning to God from a life of crime, drink or simple disbelief, Catherine felt cheated. That was something she had never been given the opportunity to do and she envied them. Always having known He was there lacked the excitement others felt in discovering God for themselves.

Now, newly signed up for The Army while doubting God's existence filled her with such guilt she felt worse than any criminal or drunk.

Catherine told no one of her doubts. In the past she'd always felt free to discuss every subject and problem with her parents. But feeling so wicked at questioning her faith – or lack of it – she declared the subject taboo.

She was convinced that if her parents ever suspected her guilty secret, it would break their hearts. The shock may even kill them. As for the General ever finding out? Well, the effect of that might just have killed Catherine herself.

And there were the other children to consider. Being the eldest, she was always held up to them as a shining example and they thought she was wonderful. This only added to her torment. It seemed so false to be guiding

30

them into believing and accepting what she herself couldn't.

Oh, what an achievement for Satan! He must have danced with joy to recruit Catherine Booth Booth, grand-daughter of The Salvation Army founders – they who shook the tambourine 'in the face of the Devil' defying him to come forth.

Oddly enough, because she doubted his existence, Catherine often went on her knees and asked God for guidance in finding Him. Then she would argue with herself 'Why pray to God when I don't believe in Him in the first place?'

Still she persevered. Her parents, grandparents and millions of believers couldn't be wrong, she reasoned. There must be an answer. But where to find it? Catherine knew she must work it out for herself and, in searching for the truth, she studied the Bible more intently than ever.

In 1882, the year before Catherine was born, some eager young Army girls had gone to work in America. Salvation Army officers don't need to be intellectual or well educated. It is their compassion and the calibre of person that matters. But in that particular instance, Bramwell worried over their lack of years, worldly experience and Army training. To overcome any recurrence of that, he established in Clapton a Training Home for Women.

Eventually, in 1903, the time arrived for Catherine, then nineteen, to take up residence there. Her leaving home caused a tremendous upheaval in the lives of the entire family. The children were growing up but Wycliffe, the youngest, was still only seven and for so long Catherine had been their second mother.

Although Clapton was only a few miles away it seemed as though Catherine was leaving for the other side of the world and they would never meet again. On May 19th,

31

the day of her departure, the family went for a long walk together through the fields and woods behind the Homestead. They commented on the new spring growth around them, reminisced on the past and shed many tears.

The training home accommodated thirty women – or lasses, as they were affectionately termed – for each training session, and the course lasted six months. At the end of that time, a 'cadet' gained the rank of Lieutenant and was posted to a corps to become Second in Command. Alternatively, she could stay on for a further six months as Sergeant before leaving to Captain a corps.

Catherine knew she was expected to stay the full course and become an officer in charge of a corps or citadel – a post which meant conducting dedications, marriages and funerals. How she dreaded having to officiate at such impressive ceremonies far away from her own environment and the love and support of her family.

On their arrival at the training home, the cadets were greeted by the Colonel who first made some jokes and teased the young 'lasses' a bit about their untidy hair and explained how to tie the floppy ribbons in order to keep their bonnets on straight. This put them at their ease before she got down to the serious business of telling them what was involved in becoming a cadet.

Perhaps the most daunting thing was being told they would spend ten minutes each day praying for the new officers in the field – those who had just completed their training – as their prayers would be greatly needed.

The rights and wrongs of dress were among the first lessons. No jewellery could be worn except for engagement and wedding rings. Watches were permitted but only if they were unadorned by silver or gold and not seen except when being consulted for the time. Hair must be neat but not worn in any stylish way, and the uniform was not to be altered to adapt to a more fashionable appearance.

They were given a Drill Book containing five hundred pages of *Rules and Regulations* to study. This covered every aspect of their lives from general behaviour to how to perform a marriage ceremony.

They would be taught how to conduct meetings; how not to let their nervousness show when faced with unpleasant situations; how to treat and encourage converts – particularly how to be tactful if their testimony went on for too long and they needed to be stopped.

They would have Bible lessons.

Every weekend they would be sent into the pubs – often alone – selling The Army's paper, *War Cry*.

They would be told how to tend to people in need of practical help as well as spiritual, such as a bereaved parent, a deserted husband, an abused wife or ill-treated children.

They were introduced to the officers salute; raising the right hand to the shoulder with the index finger pointing heavenwards. This is not meant as an act of admiration for the recipient but to indicate that they are both travelling the same route. It is also the direction in which they aim to send the souls they are intent on saving.

Perhaps the most surprising rule was to remind cadets of their status. In a society which viewed women as inferior beings, they must never forget they were of equal rank to all men and, within The Salvation Army, it was very likely they would at times hold higher rank and men would be subservient to them.

As evidence of this, officers would only be allowed to marry other officers and even then it would be frowned upon if a woman officer married one of a lower rank than herself.

Weddings could be conducted by either sex. The ceremonies begin with Army bands playing rousing tunes, and everyone wearing full uniform. The bride, wearing a cream or white and crimson sash over her uniform, appears without her bonnet. One of the vows is that their home will become an Army headquarters for all seeking help, comfort and advice. After the wedding-ring has been placed upon the bride's finger, the presiding officer will pronouce them:

'. . . man and wife together. Whom God hath joined together, let no man put asunder.'

The solemn ceremony will be followed by a grand march of guests through the street and, afterwards, a great feast.

Apart from Army officer training there would be some academic education and the cadets would also be taught household management. This included dusting, sweeping and scrubbing floors; cooking and serving meals.

Catherine's first requirement was to go and pick out her scrubbing-brush for scouring the dining-hall floor each day. Her choice was one with the hardest and shortest bristles and, as it had lost a piece of its base, it was possible to turn it on end when dealing with some particularly grimy or greasy area. It worked splendidly and after each day's work, to ensure she could always claim the same brush, Catherine carefully hid it in the broom-cupboard.

The 'Garrison' — as the cadets called the training home — was housed in an old building with long corridors sectioned off to make small rooms housing one person. After the spacious rooms at the Homestead, Catherine felt cramped in her little 'cell'. Still, it did give her privacy to weep unobserved.

The tears continued for a long time with flowers and letters of woe passing between the family daily. But, despite the sadness, there was also a sense of fulfilment. Bramwell and Florence were pleased their dear daughter was taking the path they'd prayed she would, and Catherine felt once more that she was doing what she 'ought'.

She had expected to be treated just like everyone else at the training home. However, when the other cadets realised Catherine was William Booth's granddaughter, rather than befriend her, they showed her much deference and tended to avoid her. This only added to her loneliness and sadness.

Nevertheless, in spite of – or maybe because of – her misery, she worked so hard that within three weeks she had earned a stripe and was made an 'orderly'. At the end of the first six months she was made 'Publications Sergeant'; entrusted with the distribution of the three Army magazines.

One of her worst duties during training was having to stand alone on street corners, trying to attract the attention of passers-by. This meant either singing – her weakest attribute – shaking the tambourine or raising her voice to testify, what weren't really, her beliefs.

At such times Catherine wished she was a reformed criminal or drunk, thus making her testimony more credible, *even for herself*.

Her greatest joy came one evening while selling the *War Cry* in a public house in a very rough area of London. A place where people were afraid to walk alone after dark. One customer remarked that, 'The General is taking advantage of your youth. He'd do better to send his own family to do his work in such places.' Forgetting all thoughts of shyness, and with eyes shining, Catherine proudly announced in a voice for everyone to hear, 'I am the General's granddaughter'.

But there was no joy the night a customer in another pub asked her to pray for him. Without thinking, Catherine went on her knees there and then to pray. This 'created a bad impression and was bad for business', said the landlord as he roughly grabbed hold of her and threw her out on to the street.

Although run with the precision of military army

training, life at the Garrison wasn't all solemnity. On one Open Day when the Booth family came to visit, Wycliffe brought his big sister a white mouse for company. That night she settled down to sleep with the tiny animal softly snuggled into the hollow of her throat. But the following morning, for sheer mischief she simply couldn't resist taking it into the classroom to see the reaction of the other cadets and their training officer. For a time all was peace until her pet roused itself and peered round the room. As soon as it was spotted, some burst into laughter while others shrieked and would have made for the door until they remembered they were trainee Army Officers and must keep calm in all situations. Later they came to accept cadet Booth's mouse – and its owner's mischievous streak.

All the while Catherine continued to study the Bible, seeking an end to her doubts until finally she understood where the fault lay. It wasn't in God. It wasn't in herself. It was Satan, that old adversary of all Christians, who had planted the seeds of doubt in her mind.

Catherine was furious. She had never believed herself capable of such anger and how she berated him. 'How dare you?' she demanded of the old enemy.

Salvationists refuse to believe that *God* sends people to Hell. By following the Devil's ways they choose to go there. Every lost soul brings sorrow and heartache to God. The Army's great mission is to save as many for Him as possible.

With her renewed faith, Catherine waged into the war with fists flying. For the rest of her life she talked to the Devil as often as she talked to God, always reminding him of how he had failed in his evil scheme. 'You thought you'd won my soul. Well, you didn't and you jolly well won't win any others if I have anything to do with it.'

There was still one element of doubt in her mind though – not as to whether God existed but regarding the purpose for some of the things He did. There was pain, sorrow and, worst of all, death. Why?

In the end, she decided that God knew best and accepted His ways for the future. After all, she reasoned, in order to use a spade, you don't need to know how it is made – and Catherine frequently used a spade in the garden.

Just as in childhood, illness plagued Catherine and she missed much of her training. Still, she always made up the lost time, struggling on to complete her full year's course and graduating as a Captain. As the end of the training period neared an air of eager anticipation over-took everyone.

Some of those due to leave were concerned only with buying and stitching yellow braid on to their new uniforms thus denoting their rank and successful 'graduation'; one that would take them out into the field of battle. But Catherine's mind was filled with apprehension. If leaving home in the first place was upsetting, she now faced something positively traumatic – Commissioning Day. Only then did the newly fledged officer learn to which part of the world she would be posted.

Remembering the great globe in her grandfather's study, Catherine waited in dread to be told to which little spot she was destined. To her surprise and relief it was to the beautiful city of Bath. Nothing could have pleased her more although she would stoically have accepted any posting she was given. Among her luggage as she packed were two items she couldn't bear to leave behind. One was the battered old scrubbing-brush, now long past its retirement; the other was her equally battered old tambourine. Catherine may have achieved the rank of Captain but she was adamant that these two worn-out items would never be far from her sight. To someone who was curious to know why she hadn't relegated them to

37

the rubbish-heap, the only place they were fit for, Catherine replied that she was keeping them 'just in case I ever forget my once lowly position'.

However, probably as a result of all her previous illness coupled with the intensive training, she fell ill again. It was six months later, in May the following year, before she took up her duties.

# Chapter 5

# *Joy and Tears*

At one graduation the General attended he'd laughingly ended his congratulatory speech with the words, 'I sentence you all to hard labour for the rest of your natural lives'.

This *joke* was quoted repeatedly over the years but now his granddaughter was beginning to understand the implication of those words – even if they had been spoken in a lighthearted moment. An officer's life was 'hard labour' compared with that of a cadet because added to the physical work was all the responsibility coupled with the anxieties of managing the corps.

Catherine's first discovery at Bath Two Corps was that they were in debt for £50 – quite a large sum in 1905. To overcome this, when her birthday came around in July, she asked that all her presents be in cash. With this she paid off the corps debt.

It was a good thing Florence had brought her children up on a sensible diet because Catherine and her second-in-command's weekly wage was only 7/6d (37½p) each. By pooling this money they made it go further and lived on a healthy but cheap diet of fruit, nuts, vegetables, wholemeal bread, porridge and eggs.

They were entitled to three weeks holiday each year and were expected to work seven days a week, with no evenings off. Their day began at six o'clock when they did some dusting and sweeping before breakfast. Bigger cleaning chores, laundry and shopping were done at

39

various times in the week. Cooking was shared, alternating daily. This also staggered the time between them for their quiet half hour alone with the Bible, making certain one was always free to attend to unexpected callers and unforeseen emergencies – domestic or otherwise.

Every day they cycled miles, up and down the steep streets and the hills outside the city to attend open-air meetings, visit pubs, prisons and hospitals. They gave instruction sessions for 'young soldiers' and those newly saved, and visited the homes of the sick to nurse, cook, clean, launder and care for their young children. Back at the corps there was letter writing, columns to be written for the magazines, office administration and accounts to be kept, household chores to be done.

There never seemed enough time to do it all – and yet it got done. At night they were so tired and fell asleep so quickly that the next morning they couldn't remember getting into bed the previous night.

Being shy and timid didn't help Catherine at all. She felt so embarrassed when taking converts' testimonies at meetings, and asking her audience 'Have you been saved?' Conducting dedications, weddings and funerals terrified her.

Nevertheless, honouring her grandfather's orders to do better than her best, she made an excellent leader even if, by disposition, she wasn't a natural leader.

In 1906 when he was seventy-seven and with his eyesight failing, the General embarked on a strenuous month-long tour. This took in one hundred towns, attending one hundred and twenty-five meetings and making speeches at every one of them. In Devon he called in at Dartmoor Prison bringing the word of God to all the hardened criminals who had been exhorted to 'Abandon Hope All Ye Who Enter Here'.

A year after her grandfather's example of his own

maxim to do better than one's best, France became the destination for Captain Catherine Booth's second posting. She was twenty-three and although it may seem young to hold responsibility of a foreign citadel, at that time most of The Army's leaders were aged between sixteen and twenty.

When she was a baby, Florence had once taken Catherine to visit her dearest friend, Bramwell's sister, Catherine II, who was working in France. While she was there, another dedication was held for the infant and afterwards it was always assumed she would spend some time working in that country.

Of course, Catherine didn't want to leave Britain and half wished she'd never learned the French language because that had made her the obvious choice to go. Added to homesickness, crossing the channel also made her terribly sea sick. All her life, any mode of transport caused her travel sickness.

Happily, that posting didn't last as long as she'd feared. Eighteen months later she was back at Clapton. This time it was as a training officer and, as an added bonus, amongst the newer cadets were Mary and Miriam, her two younger sisters.

Pleased though she was to be home, Catherine didn't take very kindly to one of her first assignments – playing a concertina and a barrel-organ with a monkey in the streets to raise money. Still, her sense of humour and love of fun helped overcome her reluctance and, as well as their much-needed donations, she managed to raise a lot of laughs from the public.

In the week after Catherine's return, Miriam asked for a private interview with her and confided that she was experiencing grave doubts about God's existence. Until then, with her 'second' mother out of the country, she had been unable to tell anyone.

Catherine was astounded at Miriam's sad story and was

41

immensely thankful to the Lord for recalling her to England at that time. Having experienced and finally resolved her own doubts she was now able to advise and counsel her young sister.

Her return to London also coincided with her parents' silver-wedding anniversary party at which, for the first time in months, the entire family was united.

Bramwell and Florence were so proud of their offspring. Catherine, their eldest, was a Salvation Army Captain; Mary and Miriam were Officer Cadets; Bernard, Olive and Dora were Corps Cadets and the baby of the family, twelve-year-old Wycliffe, was a Junior Soldier. How everyone revelled on that day, laughing and crying tears of joy.

Sadly, it seemed that this reunited family happiness was the Lord's way of giving them strength to face the sadness ahead.

Catherine and her father were often poorly. But it came as a shock to everyone when, just like her older sister, Miriam fell ill immediately after her graduation from Clapton. At first the doctors diagnosed appendicitis but then, on operating, discovered a huge, badly infected abscess.

Even while the family were distressed over this, Mary, too, became desperately ill with pneumonia. The doctors said she would die unless they performed a very risky lung operation. Happily her life was saved. Afterwards she needed a long convalescence to make a complete recovery. Unfortunately, though, Miriam never did fully recover and for the rest of her short life she was constantly ill.

The General was an old man now but he still insisted on working and touring. By then the young Booths had outgrown the awe they felt for him as children and freely returned the love he showered upon them.

One morning in the winter of 1912, aged eighty-two and almost blind, he fell down the stairs of his home.

This was the end, everyone thought. The shock coupled with the intense cold weather would surely kill him. But resilient as ever, just one week later he embarked upon a tour of Scandinavia. By the time he arrived home, however, he was completely blind, and in the May he underwent surgery to remove a cataract from his eye. This proved too much even for his strong constitution and determination, and in the following August he died.

That year, 1912, saw many world-shattering events – the sinking of the Titanic; Captain Scott's disastrous expedition to the South Pole; China became a republic; there was a massive strike in Britain's coalfields; and, at the age of eighty-four came the death of William Booth, founder of The Salvation Army.

Until then the longest funeral procession London had ever seen was the Duke of Wellington's in 1852. Sixty years later, William Booth's funeral surpassed it. It took over an hour for his cortège to pass along each street.

Thousands of people lined the route and all traffic was brought to a halt. How far God's Army had progressed from those days when its first few members were jeered at, stoned and spat upon as they marched along.

The funeral service was held at Olympia where Her Majesty, Queen Mary, was among the 40,000 who attended.

On August 20th, when the General was 'Promoted to Glory', the national newspapers prophesied that his death would mean the end of The Salvation Army. That great show of homage proved that they couldn't have been more mistaken.

Many years earlier, William had deposited with his solicitor a sealed envelope containing a slip of paper naming his successor. Even before it was opened, everyone assumed the person chosen to be their next General would be William's son and chief-of-staff, Bramwell.

Soon after his appointment, Bramwell left for a tour of Europe, taking Florence and Catherine with him. In Russia they were shocked to learn that Salvationists there suffered terrible persecution, both from the general public and the authorities. Their meetings had to be held in secret with great care being taken to ensure that their singing wasn't heard by any opposing ears.

Catherine now saw for herself just how badly the first Salvationists had suffered, and it made her appreciate even more her grandparents' courage in founding the movement.

At the time of that tour the whole world was poised to display courage on a scale never before imagined; 1914 saw both the military armies, and The Salvation Army mustering for war. The one preparing to fight an earthly foe; the other to challenge Satan who was causing all the trouble.

On his return home, General Bramwell sent out 'troops' to survey the ugly situation in Europe. Some went to France while Mary was among those sent to Belgium.

In August of that year, while some of Bramwell's 'troops' were still in Europe, war between Britain and Germany was declared.

'It'll all be over by Christmas!' were the words on everyone's lips. But the war, which involved many other nations, dragged on for four years with appalling loss of life on both sides.

Mary's duty was going to hospitals where she wrote letters for the wounded; read and wrote letters for the blind. The most heartbreaking work was sitting holding the hands of dying men, giving words of comfort and encouragement to those who were conscious; silently praying for those beyond reach.

But within a short time, news reached England that she had been arrested for espionage.

This was ironic because the Salvationists took 'Love thine enemy' seriously, and had sympathy for Germany's bereaved parents, widows and orphans. There was a strong Salvation Army movement there. The Booth's knew its members well and felt no animosity towards either the country or her people. Alas, at such a time, that attitude didn't arouse any compassion in Britain and the Booths were heavily criticised.

Catherine was now Major and if it hadn't been for the outbreak of World War I, she might have married. But officers may only marry officers and all the able-bodied Salvation Army men were away in the midst of the conflict, tending to and praying for the wounded. The Booth children had been among the first to have officer training. Consequently, all the young men were of junior rank to them and, as on marriage a woman took her husband's rank, it was unthinkable for Major Booth to marry anyone junior to her. The few who were of equal or senior rank were quite elderly.

In a way Catherine had no regrets over this. When anyone asked why she had never married, with a twinkle in her eyes, she always replied, 'Because no one ever asked me'. But that wasn't the real story. Any man would have been compared to her father whom she thought perfect. And, as her life had been dedicated to God, had she met a man who measured up to Bramwell and had loved him and their children as much as her mother loved hers, she may have neglected that dedication. And wasn't she to be Bramwell's successor – the future General of God's own Army?

Due to the absence of so many men, more and more women officers were needed and the training home began filling up with extra cadets, and Catherine was plunged into a situation which demanded great self assurance – something she'd never had. Amazingly, from somewhere deep within, came the spirit and fortitude she had never dreamed herself capable of.

Whenever anyone grumbled at not liking a particular task or not being able to do it, Catherine would tell her, 'Don't be so foolish! You're here for training. If you are only going to do what you like doing or find easy, then that wouldn't be training.'

However, with this firmness went sympathy, particularly to the shy or the homesick. Major Catherine Booth well remembered how she felt when first entering the training home. It was a Spartan life even in those days when every penny had to be counted. Now there was the added worry of war and, whether rich or poor, a shortage of everything.

They were depressing times but Catherine, 'always refused to acknowledge *the blues* because they're catching'. Instead she strove to keep everyone cheerful.

# Chapter 6

# *War and More Tears*

Some cadets found Major Booth difficult to get to know. Yet maybe it was they who were in awe of her because Catherine never distanced herself from her trainees.

Two things which should have shed any doubts about that were: No 1, the old battered and worn out tambourine she had so defiantly shaken in the face of the Devil during her training period. And, No 2, her scrubbing brush – the one used to scour the training home dining-room floor in her own cadet days. Both now held pride of place on her office wall, 'Just in case I'm ever tempted to forget my once lowly position'.

On one occasion when a new cadet entered the office for the first time, she found the scrubbing brush lying on the floor. Horrified that anyone should have been so careless as to leave the offending article in Major's room, she quickly picked it up and took it down to the basement to put in with the rubbish. Fortunately, Catherine entered her office, noticed the precious heirloom was missing and ordered an immediate search of the building. The brush was rescued just in time.

From thirty cadets at each six-monthly session, the number had grown to nearly four hundred and Catherine was determined to know them all individually. As Major, she was given her own house next to the home and so, for a month at a time, she had twenty of the girls living with her. This smaller number was better to deal with rather than trying to 'break through a solid lump'.

Goodness, love – and mischief – shone from her eyes. At the close of one sticky, miserable day during a summer heatwave, she surprised everyone by suggesting, 'Why don't you take off your shoes and stockings, go into the garden and run about in the grass?'

Like carefree children in the cool evening air they danced around and chased each other, playing 'tick'.

On another occasion when the cadets were sitting around, tired and downcast after a particularly hard day, they were told a gypsy woman was at the door and would like to tell their fortunes.

'A gypsy fortune teller at the Salvation Army Training Home? How dare she?' they asked, but filled with curiosity, they asked her to be brought in.

In came the gypsy who soon had them all roaring with laughter as she proceeded to mumble the most ridiculous predictions. It was only when someone remarked, 'What a pity Major isn't here' and they heard a stifled giggle from within the gypsy's head shawl that they realised Major was there! Such diversions were necessary at that time. It was World War I with Zeppelin bombing raids over London.

Almost nightly, clad in dressing-gowns or draped in blankets, the girls scurried downstairs to the home's air-raid shelter – the basement dining-room. They stumbled along, falling over each other in the darkness as no light must be shown for fear of helping the enemy sight a target. Often they bumped into Catherine, still struggling into her clothes having wasted no time in racing across from her own house to be with them.

After spending the night in the shelter, the following morning would see them out helping those who'd lost their homes and loved ones during the raid.

Throughout those years, even when there were no air-raids, Catherine would often stay up right through the night, replying to letters from those who sought her advice on problems. Sometimes it was to write letters of sympathy to those whose menfolk had been 'killed in action' or were 'missing believed killed'.

Only now was she beginning to understand fully why the cadets spent ten minutes each day praying for newly fledged officers in the field. At Bath Two Corps, and later in France, she had encountered innumerable problems and battled on, almost alone, trying to solve them.

But she now realised that most young officers wrote 'home' for counselling or to air their grievances and doubts. Day after day letters poured into her office until, in the end, she was writing a line here, a line there whenever she could snatch a free moment. But her *free* moments were getting less and less all the time, and with so many officers graduating, more and more letters arrived. Amongst the many problems, the most repetitive were:

I'm so disillusioned in my work I'm tempted to leave The Army.

The townspeople don't like us.

I'm overworked and feel too tired to carry on.

Some of the converts go back on their pledges and revert to their old ways.

My Lieutenant/Captain is unhelpful.

In desperation Catherine appealed to her father for advice. Bramwell wisely suggested that, as in many instances her 'lasses' problems tended to duplicate, she should write an 'open letter' to them in each monthly issue of The Army's publication, *The Officer*. That way she could answer everybody without sending individual letters.

The first training college letter – which really amounted to an article – came from Switzerland while Catherine was visiting her sick sister, who was convalescing in a sanatorium there. In the middle of a sweet scented pine forest in a neutral country, far away from the horrors of war, she sat beside Miriam's bed in a picturesque chalet and wrote to:

My Dear W – – –

I have thought so much of you since I saw you and . . .

The letter went on giving guidance, understanding, sympathy and hope for her 'lasses'. From then on, over the next four years, Catherine produced a similar letter for each issue of *The Officer*. And although no one was ever named, each reader felt the letter was dedicated to her alone.

Over and over again one theme recurred, urging the officers never to become blasé in their work. Although they might provide the same service a hundred times, they must always remember that it could be the first time for those they were tending.

New converts should not simply be accepted, have an Army ribbon pinned on them and then be left to get on with their new found faith. They must be encouraged and never be allowed to feel forgotten. Always have a kind word of encouragement, she advised. Ask about their families, their work, their health. Go to their homes. Invite them to march with you and repeat their testimonies at various venues. Let them *know* their worth to mankind, to the Army and most of all to God.

To the tired and overworked she suggested they take their annual holiday without delay, and that it should be considered by the title it had in the early Salvation Army days – 'on rest'.

Get plenty of sleep. It is more important than food and drink.

Go to bed early and rise as late as you like.

Get out in the fresh air as often as possible. Even if it is cold you can wrap up warm.

Read *recreational* books; detective stories if you like them but definitely not those concerned with work or self improvement.

And give your mind a rest. Let it wander and think its own thoughts.

Also, get out of uniform but not into anything too worldly. You can always pin an Army brooch in your clothes to show who and what you are.

To those finding difficulty working with their partner, she reminded *both them and the partner* of their duties towards each other.

Always show respect to *all* other officers.

Take an interest in their personal lives and their families.

Show gratitude for any little act of kindness or help.

You will not necessarily agree with your colleague's opinions but in public you must always appear to.

If you must speak of their faults do it in private and with discretion.

At Clapton, the young cadets worst experience was when an arms factory exploded killing men, women and children in nearby houses.

As usual, The Salvation Army was among the first on the scene. But these weren't hardened campaigners. They were young, half-trained girls, inexperienced in death, maimings and destruction. Thanks to Catherine's strict leadership, and her calmness, everyone set to work without hesitation. Even the most timid and squeamish toiled alongside the other rescue teams.

They gave out hot drinks and consoled those standing around surveying the wreckage of their homes and waiting to know the fate of their families. Some went to the makeshift mortuary to give comfort to survivors as they were called on to identify the bodies of their loved ones; one young widow had been left with five small children.

An old man nearing eighty was so in shock that he didn't seem to realise his house had collapsed around him save for the one remaining wall where he sat by the fireside with his two cats.

In the midst of such tragedy and horror, Catherine was really proud of her 'lasses' that night.

Shortly after that disaster in 1917, and only three weeks from Christmas, she was faced with another tragedy. This time a personal one. Miriam died.

A few years earlier, Catherine had grieved over the General's death but had been able to accept it. At eighty-four, he had lived a long, full, useful and happy life.

But poor Miriam had barely begun to live. For years she had suffered terribly. She was only thirty and was engaged to be married. Nevertheless, Catherine didn't question God's reason for this. She simply acknowledged that He had one.

Without even asking Him to, God had already made provision for easing Catherine through her sorrow in His own way. As the New Year of 1918 dawned, she was going to be posted – away from the memories the training home held of Miriam when she had been a cadet.

Major Catherine Booth wrote in her monthly letter for *The Officer* that she was leaving the training college and that this would be her last letter to her 'lasses'. She told them of how, in January 1914, she had sat beside Miriam's bed while writing the first letter. And now this was the evening before 'we lay her dear body to rest'.

At thirty-four, Catherine was to become Under Secretary for Europe at International Headquarters in London. This was an important appointment at any time, but with war raging on the continent, it carried many more responsibilities – and problems – than usual.

Differences in politics, race, colour or creed were never observed by God's Army. People were people. The only true enemy of man was Satan. Therefore, Salvationists felt no hatred for Germany or her people.

Sadly, because of this attitude, for the first time in decades, The Salvation Army met with hostility – even from their greatest supporters.

When they donated an ambulance, bedding and medical supplies for the war wounded, both the War Office and the Red Cross declined to accept them at first. They claimed that, as The Salvation Army symbolised God and had too-Christian an outlook, their gifts wouldn't be acceptable to the men fighting in Europe.

Meanwhile, God's Army continued to fight its own war in Britain against poverty and depression. They campaigned for food and shelter for the war widowed and orphaned: the homeless, the sick, the poor. They fought for the souls of drunks; down-and-outs and sinners everywhere. They visited hospitals and prisons, traced missing persons and raced to every emergency with hot drinks, blankets and any other assistance they could provide.

In her exalted position, Catherine was able to discover that Mary's trial as a British spy had been dismissed. She was also kept informed of her sister's whereabouts. Transferred from prison camp to prison camp, Mary was finally interned for the duration of the war.

In every camp she was sent to she led rousing songs and read the Bible to her fellow prisoners. When the German guards remonstrated with her, Mary, who spoke fluent German, argued, 'What do you mean, forbidding me to read the Bible? All the Germans I know read the Bible. Don't *you* read it?'

After that she had no trouble. She even wrote to her mother asking her to somehow get some *German* translated Bibles out to the camp for her to distribute to her captors.

Eventually, after four years of unimaginable horror, on the November 11th, 1918, the war ended.

And although the hostilities between Germany and the rest of the world weren't easily forgotten, as celebrations went on everywhere, those between the public and The Salvation Army were.

When a huge procession marched to meet London's Lord Mayor at his official home, The Mansion House, Major Catherine Booth was among many other officers to receive his thanks for all their good works.

# Chapter 7

# *War on Distress*

Within weeks of that rejoicing the world was hearing that in Germany, men, women and children were starving to death.

Understandably, many people – especially those who had lost loved ones – were bitter and would have left the defeated foe to its fate. However, one lady, Eglantyne Jebb, thought that the children at least should be cared for. But only having £10 to offer, she began asking for donations and was immediately arrested for treason. Fortunately, the publicity of her arrest highlighted her story of sickness and famine. People began to see reason – as far as German *children* were concerned anyway. Money began pouring in and the case against her was dismissed.

With The Salvation Army's knowledge of charitable work and of Europe itself, they were among the first to offer assistance. As Catherine was Under-Secretary for European Affairs she was chosen to go to Germany to assist in distributing the desperately needed supplies from Eglantyne Jebb's new organisation – today famous as the Save the Children Fund – which gave them £5,000.

Under Catherine's direction, Germany's own Salvation Army set to allocating clothes, medical supplies and food. The most precious commodity was condensed milk, which fed babies, toddlers and older children.

However, experience had taught Catherine that some children wouldn't actually receive the milk. Uncaring

55

parents would sell it for cigarettes and other goods. So, at her suggestion, rules were made whereby:

1. To obtain a tin of milk, each child must take vitamins – a dose of cod-liver oil.
2. To receive a second tin, the first tin must be returned when empty.
3. A Salvation Army officer must be permitted to visit the child's home. This mostly to see if any other kind of help could be given, both practical and spiritual.

After doing such good work in Germany, from then on Catherine was sent to Finland, Sweden, Russia, Belgium, Holland, and France to visit the people and their Salvation Armies. But how she loathed travelling with its inevitable accompanying sickness.

Crossing the channel was torture and more than once a stretcher was needed to carry her ashore when the ferry docked. Visiting remote villages she would have to cross rocky terrain on mules, each step making her stomach churn.

On a visit to Holland, she vomited so much during the journey that on arrival she suddenly suffered a very serious lung haemorrhage. The doctors were sure Catherine couldn't survive. Afterwards she remembered little of her illness except thinking that she had reached the end of her days and started quarrelling with God. It was His fault, she told Him. Hadn't she done everything He'd asked of her – including making all those dreadful journeys?

Gradually, she began recovering – albeit being ordered to lie completely still. She was unable to wash herself and was forbidden to take deep breaths or eat anything that needed chewing for fear that using her chest muscles might start the haemorrhage off again.

On returning to England she was advised by her doctor to 'go and live among pine trees for the sake of your lungs'. This usually meant Scotland or Switzerland but Catherine was fortunate in knowing of such a place quite close to home – Finchamstead near Wokingham in Berkshire. There she bought a delightful little cottage and moved in for the rest of her long convalescence during which time she made friends with God again.

It hadn't been His fault at all but that old menace's, Satan. No wonder she was always ill when travelling. That would be his way of making her give in and stay at home. Well, she had no intention of surrendering even though it took her four years to recover completely.

In 1926, Catherine, now aged forty-three, was fit and ready for work again. By this time she had been promoted to the rank of Colonel and on resuming her duties was put in charge of women's social welfare; work which Catherine's own mother, Florence, had carried on from her mother-in-law, the Army Mother.

It consisted mainly of giving shelter and succour to the homeless or to battered wives. Of having arrangements with the magistrates and the police whereby convicted criminals were taken from the police courts and straight into Army Homes to prevent them serving prison sentences. Other women came directly from prison after their sentences were served. They stayed with the Army for three months during which time they would be rehabilitated: given instructions on child care; good housekeeping and how to lead honest, useful lives. In return they were expected to keep the Home clean and attend regular meetings and interviews with the officers to let them see how they were progressing. There was also one other condition. By their own charitable efforts, they must raise a sum of £3 towards the residential expense of another unfortunate. This responsibility for others' welfare was often alien to some of the women who went through life thinking only of themselves. It made them look into their own hearts.

Of course, not all the women under The Army's care met Catherine personally because it was a nationwide – or rather world-wide – concern. But those in the London shelters were often surprised to be told that 'the Colonel is coming tomorrow'.

It wasn't unusual for her to turn up very early in the morning in all kinds of weather, and when she told them she'd come for breakfast, the women were amazed. During the meal she would chat cosily to them, asking about their lives and their families. This would lead to their future and advice on how to change their past ways. If they genuinely wanted to, with God's help, she would do everything in her power to help them. For those in need of shelter through no fault of their own, the fact that Colonel Catherine Booth, granddaughter of The Salvation Army founder, was sitting at table, eating with them and showing such a personal interest gave more hope and encouragement towards self respect than any lecture.

No one was ever judged or criticised. Instead, they were encouraged to judge and criticise themselves. And those who knew nothing of God and His love were introduced to Him.

There was great joy when a thief, drunkard, child beater, or runaway wife and mother reformed her ways. Most of the women were reunited with their parents or their husbands and children. Many made return visits to The Army taking their families with them. This really made the work worthwhile. But above all, the greatest rejoicing was when a pentitent accepted God, and the Devil was cheated out of yet another soul.

Sadly though, there were occasions when all their efforts, goodwill and prayers came to nought. Sometimes Catherine was so despondent she was tempted to think;

'Why bother praying for her? It's hopeless. She'll never be any different'.

Then she would stop thinking of *her* as a person and consider only the woman's soul that was so in need of salvation. Consequently her faith in humanity would be restored and her efforts renewed.

In 1926, when Catherine resumed work, Bramwell celebrated his seventieth birthday which was marked by a big Salvation Army gathering in London. Like his father before him, Bramwell commanded great respect and affection which was reflected in the many greetings – including one from King George V. And like his daughter before him, he requested that all gifts be in cash. This amounted to £164,000 which was promptly donated to Army funds.

Although he was fit and well, seventy was a considerable age, particularly for someone with a weak constitution who had worked so hard throughout his life. As no one is immortal, some sensibly looked ahead to when Bramwell would no longer be with them. During the celebration they made discreet enquiries regarding his thoughts on retirement only to receive their answer two weeks later when he and Florence set off for America.

As a result, together with overwork, lack of rest and constant worry over sustaining The Salvation Army, which depended completely on charity, that strenuous American tour took its toll of Bramwell's health. Shortly after his return, although suffering flu and the fact there was a raging blizzard, he insisted on travelling to an Army meeting in Yorkshire.

Days later, on May 10th, 1928, against advice, he insisted on attending the stone-laying ceremony of his father's memorial – the International Training College for officers at Denmark Hill, in London.

No one knew that this would be Bramwell's last appearance before his adoring public.

As news of his failing health became known, a deputation of Army personnel went to ask him to retire, but Bramwell adamantly refused. His father, William, had given him the appointment. It was for the Lord to decide when he should give it up.

His refusal was followed by a meeting of the High Council, of which Colonel Catherine was a member.

When lengthy discussions were held concerning a new rule compelling retirement at sixty-five, she was displeased. When they went on to debate the form of selecting the future General, she was horrified. Couldn't Bramwell nominate his own successor as his father had before him?

The High Council sympathised with Catherine and admired her loyalty. It had been right for William, as Army founder, to choose his successor. But the time had come for change. Although, until the time of his death, no one could know officially who Bramwell had chosen, they assumed it would be his daughter. No one questioned her suitability for the appointment but if she followed her father – who had followed his – it could appear that the post was hereditary. As The Salvation Army was now a universal organisation, was it right that one person alone should choose the future leader? The High Council thought not. From then on, rather than be *selected* the General must be *elected*.

A vote was taken and by 52 to 5 the motion was carried. The five against were all members of the Booth family.

When they returned to the Homestead, Catherine went upstairs to tell her father the sad news. As she drew near to his bed she avoided looking at him. She needn't have worried. Bramwell spared her when he turned and said, 'They've had a meeting of the High Council, haven't they?'

He was deeply hurt at his enforced retirement and at

60

his father's wishes being overturned, and, in the following April, when he was made Companion of Honour, it seemed to matter little to him.

The end of Bramwell's life came quite unexpectedly a few weeks later, on June 16th, 1929 – exactly one hundred years after the birth of his parents.

King George V and Queen Mary sent messages of condolence. For two days his body 'lay in state'. And his long funeral procession was reminiscent of his father's all those years before. There were brass bands, crowds lined the streets and The Army women wore the now familiar white funeral sashes bearing the crimson crown and cross.

Edward J. Higgins, the newly elected General of The Salvation Army, was an excellent choice and no one recognised this more than Catherine. Still she grieved, not from personal disappointment but for her father, knowing how he had longed for her to be the future General. Well, that had been rendered impossible but there was one way in which she could be named as his successor.

Now aged forty-seven and still unmarried, she was obviously never going to use the extra Booth in her name. Instead she substituted it for her father's and became known as Catherine Bramwell Booth.

Devastated by his death, she found it impossible to concentrate on anything properly. To overcome this she took two years off from her duties during which she planned to write his biography.

So much had been achieved since those first days when her grandfather introduced the 'soup kitchens' to London's East End. At the time of Bramwell's 'Promotion to Glory', The Army had 16,000 citadels and corps with 26,000 officers and cadets. They were spread over seventy countries, world-wide; its members communicating in fifty different languages. There were more than a hundred children's homes as well as employment bureaux, factories, workshops and many other establishments.

By 1932, the book was completed and Catherine felt able to resume her duties as William and Bramwell would have wished. If anything, she worked harder than ever; thinking up all sorts of ways to augment The Army funds. Aware of how, in her heart, she was still deeply grieving, people remarked on how she bravely hid her sorrow.

Nothing proved this more than at one of the first meetings she conducted after her return. Standing tall and straight, with an unsmiling face she solemnly announced the next song 'Wherever He May Guide Me, No Want Shall Turn Me Back'. But then her mouth and eyes creased into mischievous laughter as she added, 'and it will be sung to the tune of – 'When The Cats Get Up In The Morning'.

In 1934 when Edward Higgins retired, her aunt, Evangeline, daughter of grandfather William Booth, succeeded him as General of The Salvation Army. This gave Catherine some comfort for, although her aunt had been *elected* to office, it would have been what The Army founder and Bramwell, his son, would have wanted.

# Chapter 8

# *Retirement? Not Quite!*

The Army was always short of funds because as their work expanded, whatever money they had was quickly dispersed.

Catherine was always endorsing fund-raising events and would never allow a social occasion to pass without broaching the subject. She actually organised parties in order to make appeals to her guests regarding the Army's hardships and needs. People were very generous and gave as much as they could. The really wealthy donated huge sums of money. One even gave a large building which was put into use as an Eventide Home – home for the aged – The Salvation Army's latest venture at that time.

As well as providing food, shelter and hope to the destitute, felons or converts, Catherine, recently promoted to Commissioner Bramwell-Booth, thought they should also tend to the old and the lonely – even those who weren't in need of practical assistance or spiritual comfort. After all, she reasoned, people could be surrounded by material luxury and have undying faith in God yet lead a miserable existence.

Some were old, infirm, physically and/or mentally handicapped. Maybe their families lived at too great distances to visit them. Maybe they'd outlived their families and friends and, because they lived alone, went for days – or weeks – without talking to or even seeing anyone. Perhaps some were *fortunate* in receiving daily visits from the District Nurse or doctor. But it wasn't the same as having some friendly face drop in simply to chat, make a cup of tea, do the shopping or a few jobs about the home.

And apart from those content to have visits from the 'lasses' in their own homes there could be others who would like to leave their home and be gathered under one roof with others their age for security and companionship. And this was how the Eventide Homes came to be established.

There were some who had spent so much time alone they had forgotten how to mix with other people and make friends but, once they were settled in, the change that came over them was amazing. Others who had given up all notion of social behaviour – personal hygiene and good manners – took a new interest in themselves and showed consideration for others. They felt safe and were always sure of a good bed, fresh laundry, wholesome food and companionship. In the evenings they would get together for sing-songs, and Catherine often joined in the merriment.

By 1939 the world was in conflict again and, within a year of World War II being declared, Catherine was once more put in charge of staff training. This time it was at the International Training College, Denmark Hill – the one built as a memorial to her grandfather and where, at the stone-laying ceremony twelve years earlier, Bramwell made his last public appearance.

Catherine was now aged fifty-six with her golden-brown hair turned to white. But that impish smile remained and her hazel eyes still held the sparkle of youth. Nevertheless, that didn't prevent illness from forcing her to relinquish the post after she had held it for precisely one month.

Throughout the war years ill health dogged her. And it wasn't until 1946, one year after the war had ended, that she was really well enough to take on such a responsible post again. Then General Osborne, the Army's latest leader, made her International Secretary for Europe – a similar appointment to the one she'd held at the beginning of World War I.

Of course, at that time Catherine had been only thirty-four. Now she was sixty-three years of age, and retirement loomed ahead. And although just having recovered from years of illness, she was once more travelling all over the continent, encountering extremes of weather conditions – intense summer heat, freezing winter cold – and always travel sick. Still, she stoically resolved that God's will must be done.

On one voyage to Finland the ship got stuck fast in ice just off the Swedish coast.

'It will take days for an ice-breaker to come and free us,' the passengers were told. On hearing this, Catherine asked the captain if she could send a telegram to those awaiting her arrival in Finland. But there were no such facilities on board. Undaunted, she dropped over the ship's side and set off on foot across the frozen sea to find a post office on a nearby island. Afterwards she had to walk all the way back to the ship. From then on she often joked about the day she 'walked on water'.

At last, July 1948 arrived and with it her sixty-fifth birthday when, according to Army ruling, she must retire.

Officially, Commissioner Catherine Bramwell Booth had completed forty-five years' work for The Salvation Army. In reality, it had been nearer sixty considering those early days at home when she spent hours folding copies of *War Cry*, *Young Soldier* and *Deliverer*. There were the times spent with the High Barnet Corps and the Band of Love, and not forgetting the years spent caring for her younger brothers and sisters while her parents were away from home on Army business.

Even after her retirement, General Osborne asked if she would stay on as advisor to them. As she was the granddaughter of the Salvation Army founder, Catherine thought it was something she *ought* to do and agreed.

That year saw her in hospital for the removal of her gall-bladder from which she made a rapid and full recovery. Oddly enough, although past retirement age, from then on she was fitter than at any other period in her life.

None of the Booth girls had married and as Florence was now eighty-seven, Catherine, Mary, Olive and Dora felt it would be nice for them all to live once more under the same roof.

The Homestead at Hadley Wood was sold along with Catherine's own home. With the money from both house sales they bought a large, and rather stately home close to the Finchamstead cottage where Catherine had lived for many years.

Hidden from view of the road, North Court stood in its own grounds overlooking picturesque countryside. It was an ideal situation for such keen gardeners as the Booths, and also for Florence, who could spend many happy hours on fine days sitting watching her daughters at work.

Thus, the four ladies settled down to peace and quiet for the rest of their days – or so they thought.

As the house was quite big, they invited some relatives and friends to share it with them. There were also servants, and – to do the heavy work – they engaged a gardener. In all, they numbered eleven. Far from being 'peaceful' it was a very lively atmosphere, full of laughter, song and an endless stream of visitors who sometimes came to tea and stayed for a week.

North Court was such a happy household that even the 'young' ones – those not yet retired – spent as much time at home as possible. Their two married brothers, together with their own families, were frequent visitors. The one sadness was that Bramwell and Miriam were missing from the family circle.

66

In the past, Catherine either never had time to read the sort of books she liked or felt she *ought* to read those that would improve her mind. Now there was time for her favourite detective stories and thrillers, but instead, she chose to *write* another book. The biography of her grandmother, Catherine Booth, co-founder of The Salvation Army.

Florence helped enormously with research, providing old posters, letters, diaries, and photographs, as well as her own cherished memories of an adored mother-in-law.

Alas that almost carefree existence lasted but a short time. With such elderly people living there, it wasn't long before there were deaths. Their first loss was one of the friends who was to be closely followed by others.

In 1956, the year of her father's birth centenary, much to her astonishment – and delight because she was so proud of Bramwell – Catherine was asked to give an interview about him on television.

Sadly, in the following year, at the age of ninety-six, Florence died. And on June 16th, 1957 – the ninety-eighth anniversary of William and Catherine Booth's wedding day and the twenty-eighth anniversary of Bramwell's death – she was laid to rest beside her beloved Bramwell.

After her mother's death, although eight years' work had gone into it, Catherine lost heart in writing her grandmother's biography and placed it in a drawer. Eventually, after offering to take over from where their mother had left off with the research, Olive persuaded her to carry on with it.

Knowing her sister when she was fired with enthusiasm, Olive stipulated that she had no intention of working after 9.30 pm. Catherine accepted this condition although she herself often wrote right through the night. But before the book was finished yet another sadness was to fall upon North Court. In 1969 Mary died at the age of eighty-four.

Catherine always sensed that her sister was too fond

of the outside world to have *chosen* Salvation Army life. Perhaps like herself, being dedicated, she had felt it was the life she *ought* to lead. If she'd ever nursed the same doubts about God that once befell Catherine and Miriam, she certainly never voiced them. As a child, when Salvationists were being persecuted, she'd told Catherine she wished that she too could be put in prison to share their misery. It didn't occur to either of them at the time that she would someday be incarcerated in a foreign prisoner-of-war camp. Her horrific experiences in Germany had left many mental scars of which she said little. Still, Catherine was happy in the knowledge that at least Mary's latter years were spent amid love and comfort.

Her grandmother's biography was eventually finished and was published in 1970, when Catherine was once more invited to be interviewed on television; this time by Magnus Magnusson. This was the year of her eighty-seventh birthday when it might be assumed that she was nearing the end of her life. Instead, 1970 was destined to be the year when the Commissioner embarked on a new lease of life.

During the interview, Catherine was so unaffected, so much her natural self, that the television audience loved her. Soon other chat-show hosts were clamouring to have her on their own shows. Although never consciously seeking the limelight, Catherine loved this opportunity to be back in action again because she had never taken kindly to being old.

'Please grant me the patience to accept it,' she asked the Lord, reminding him that, 'You decided it for me. I didn't want it.'

With even more deaths, their numbers were further depleted and the house was becoming too big for those who were left. Naturally, at their time of life, none of them wanted to move house again, so, they decided to take

68

in paying guests. This served two purposes. It brought in extra money to pay servants wages, rates, electric and other household bills. Also, it kept the house 'alive'. Catherine made sure of that.

Despite being a diagnosed diabetic – facing daily injections and a rigid diet – she acted as advisor to The Salvation Army, supervised the household, was forever writing letters and still managed to keep everyone in hoots of laughter.

To entertain the guests and keep up the family's spirit, she would use every conceivable excuse to throw a party. As well as birthdays, Christmas and New Year, they also celebrated the shortest day of the year, the longest day of the year, Leap year and anything else that turned up on the calendar.

At one party, just as all those years before at the training home, Catherine dressed up, not as a gypsy women but as 'a poor little old lady'.

In an old crinoline with back and knees bent so as not to betray her height, she entered the room. Then, to everyone's surprise, she began giving out gifts of chocolate and sweets. Only when someone caught the impish gleam in 'the little old lady's' eye did they realise who their benefactor was.

# Chapter 9

# *One Century*

Perhaps Catherine should have foreseen what lay ahead when, in 1971 at the age of eighty-eight, she was created a CBE – a Companion of the British Empire.

To receive her award from the Queen she attended Buckingham Palace with her young brother, Commissioner Wycliffe, amid an unexpected blaze of publicity. Besieged for autographs, she unceremoniously used his back as a 'desk' while signing them.

No doubt believing it would be her last public appearance, reporters and photographers surrounded the 'grand old lady'.

Confident that now she would fade into obscurity, she again prayed for patience to cope with her own approaching and inevitable infirmity. But obscurity didn't come.

Two years later saw her receiving letters and telegrams from all over the world in celebration of her ninetieth birthday. And to commemorate her great age a book of verse, which she had compiled decades earlier, was re-issued.

Surely her life was drawing to a close now, she thought. But two years later it wasn't Catherine, the eldest, but Wycliffe, the youngest Booth, who was 'Promoted to Glory'.

In 1976 Catherine received a telephone call from a TV company requesting yet another interview; this time at North Court so that viewers could see her in her own environment.

Although always nervous of speaking in public, her previous television appearance hadn't worried her because *she* couldn't see the audience. But at the prospect of inviting millions of viewers into her home, she was a trembling wreck. She fervently asked God, not for patience, but to prevent her from saying the wrong things in front of the camera and 'putting my foot in it'.

This prayer was answered by her giving so good an interview that she was elected Best Speaker of the Year for 1977 by the Guild of Professional Toastmasters. How odd, she thought with a chuckle, that toastmasters who are always exhorting people to drink should make an award to someone from The Salvation Army knowing how bitterly opposed they are to alcohol. And as it was actually 1978 when she received the award – a rosewood gavel set on a silver plinth – she quipped, 'And I haven't said a word *this* year'.

For the presentation the press, radio and television reporters were invited. The room was crowded and Catherine took advantage of what she called 'her captive audience' to ask if they had faith in God. Her question made some squirm a bit but she was determined to speak her mind.

After a lengthy speech during which she asked everyone who was without faith in God to look within themselves, she asked if they had any questions.

'Yes,' piped up one voice, 'Commissioner Catherine Bramwell Booth, do you know that you have the gift of the gab?'

With eyes twinkling, she replied, 'Oh, yes I do. All the Booths have.'

In 1980 she was asked to speak at the National Free Church Womens' Council. Queen Elizabeth, the Queen Mother, who celebrated her own eightieth birthday that year, was among the audience, and afterwards they had quite a lengthy conversation.

In 1981, when Catherine was ninety-eight, she was given the Humanitarian Award by the Variety Clubs International which was presented to her by the Duke of Kent.

She appeared on television in the Russell Harty Show and was twice a guest on Michael Parkinson's show. On one occasion, he asked if she didn't think Christmas had become too commercialised. To his surprise she told him that it wasn't such a bad thing to have everyone racing about looking for presents for, after all, they were thinking of others rather than themselves.

With all this publicity, people from her past – who had assumed her long since dead – began writing to her recalling experiences they had shared. Strangers wrote to tell her what The Army had done for them. There was so much correspondence, The Salvation Army sent a secretary to North Court to help answer all her 'fan mail' – both the official and the personal.

Catherine dictated the hundreds of letters to be typed but always added a handwritten paragraph at the bottom. But when she developed rheumatism in her shoulders and the simple effort of picking up a pen caused great pain, the doctor said she must stop writing those personal notes or she would aggravate the complaint and be unable to use her arms at all.

Far from being retired, Catherine – in the old age she detested – found herself as busy and as much, if not more so, in demand as ever. No longer did she pray for patience to cope with age but for the energy to cope with her newly acquired hectic lifestyle.

It was amusing that people seemed to think she was ageless and were still sending invitations for her to give lectures or simply talk to them about The Salvation Army. These requests would have involved her travelling, not only the length of Britain but in Europe also, and sometimes to other parts of the world. The invitations were politely declined with a gentle reminder that Commissioner Catherine Bramwell Booth was nearing her centenary and rarely left her home.

Reporters and photographers were always telephoning seeking interviews for articles that appeared in newspapers and magazines world-wide, but in this her 'young' sisters were very strict. The interviewers may not arrive earlier than 11a.m., just in time for coffee before meeting the Commissioner.

North Court stood at the end of a long drive skirted by trees and gardens. On entering the hallway, guests were confronted by a bust of General Bramwell Booth and a faded, old Salvation Army drum together with various other mementoes of the family and its past.

After coffee and instructions from the *younger ones* not to tire her too much, Catherine would join them. All three sisters would be in full Army uniform leaving the photographer or journalist feeling rather overwhelmed in their presence. However, after a few minutes, Colonel Olive and Senior Major Dora would leave the room and the interview would begin.

Catherine's mind and speech were incredibly clear with poignant memories of childhood, her parents and grand-parents being recalled as though events had happened only recently. It wouldn't be long, however, before the interviewers found the tables had turned and they had become the interviewees. She wanted to know everything about them; from their place of origin to whether they were married or not. How many constituted their family? Did they have faith in God? Did they pray together?

At last it would be time for lunch after which the interview would probably come to an end and the Commissioner would retire for her afternoon rest. But if *her* interview of a reporter had lasted any considerable time, they would have to resume in order for the reporter to get all the information required.

As 1983 – the year of her hundredth birthday –
dawned, preparations were put into operation months
before the event. Salvation Army officers were sent from
abroad to interview her for their country's *War Cry*.
More reporters than ever arrived daily at North Court,
and a television interview with Malcolm Muggeridge was
arranged.

Her sisters, Lt Colonel Olive and Senior Major Dora,
were extremely concerned when they learned that a
massive celebration party was being organised at the
Cumberland, one of the grandest hotels in London. When
they heard it would be followed by a Salvation Army
meeting in Regent Hall they were frantic with worry.

Travelling had always made Catherine ill and she had
rarely left home during the past year. With the added
excitement over her one-hundredth-birthday celebrations,
they wondered if she would survive it.

When the great day arrived Olive and Dora took charge
by keeping reporters at bay and bullying Catherine into
resting in preparation for the evening ahead. Even then,
some Army officials bearing good wishes and gifts simply
had to be received. Then there was the presentation of
the traditional greetings telegram from the Queen.

That night as she entered the foyer of the Cumberland
Hotel, far from looking a little, frail centenarian – as
many had expected – her guests saw Commissioner Catherine Bramwell Booth walk tall and erect. Her eyes shone
from a bright little apple of a face as she gazed about
her with pride – pride in her heart for William, Bramwell
and The Salvation Army.

The hotel chef presented her with an enormous cake
made in the shape of The Salvation Army badge and the
party got under way. Olive and Dora kept a watchful eye
on her but Catherine was enjoying herself too much to
notice.

Later at Regent Hall when she was given another huge

74

cake her eyes lit up to outshine its hundred candles. Out of concern for her years, someone asked if she would care to 'blow out just one of the candles'. Catherine glared at him, took a deep breath and blew out ten.

This was followed by the reading out of some of her greetings cards and telegrams. The telegram she'd received from the Queen that morning was read out to the guests. There was also a telegram from the Queen Mother, and several from abroad.

There followed many speeches of gratitude for all that Catherine had done for The Army. But when her brother, Bernard, went on for what she considered far too long, Catherine interrupted him saying, 'Can't we sing the One Hundredth Psalm now?' Which they promptly did.

At last the meeting was coming to an end and Catherine stood up to thank everyone for coming. She scrutinised the rows of people seated in front of her, bright summer clothes standing out starkly against the dark Army uniforms. After a moment she declared, 'There are too many Salvationists here! Aren't there any sinners present? As long as there are sinners the world will need The Salvation Army.'

When Olive thought her sister had been on her feet for long enough, she tugged at her sleeve and suggested she sit down. Catherine shrugged her away. A minute or so later there was another tug at her sleeve. 'I'll sit down in a minute, Olive,' Catherine said impatiently and carried on with her speech. Eventually, she finished speaking and requested that everyone sing 'Give To Jesus, Glory'. Then she turned to Olive, smiled and said, '*Now* I'll sit down!'

As the ceremonies drew to a close she asked for the red, yellow and blue Salvation Army flag to be brought on stage. Under that flag, at the age of fifteen, she had signed in as a soldier. Now, she wanted to sign off the day's events by singing the song she sang on that day eighty-five years earlier – 'I'll Be True, Lord, To Thee'. Three days later a private family party was held at North Court. Olive and Dora had rounded up every Booth they could find. The in-laws, nieces, nephews and cousins numbered eighty and some didn't only not know each other – they didn't know of each other's existence.

As on most of her other birthdays, Olive and Dora requested that all gifts be in money which they insisted Catherine spent on herself – for a change.

With some of it Catherine bought a colour television set but, true to character, it was for her sisters.

# Chapter 10

# *Back to God*

No matter how loved a person is, no matter how vital they are, no one is immortal. And at one hundred years old, the inevitable had to be faced. Catherine wouldn't live for very much longer.

From that wonderful birthday everyone attempted to restrain her – a little, but there were still a number of commitments such as the television interviews ahead though.

One interview became very famous due to her remarks as it was drawing to a close. 'God be with you,' she said to her admiring audience. There followed a slight pause during which she stared at them and then added, 'And He will be, whether you want Him to or not.' How the people loved her. Their applause and cheers were almost as loud as the Hallelujahs on that morning in 1883 when Florence dedicated and gave her baby daughter back to God.

During 1984 Bernard was 'Promoted to Glory'. But still Catherine held her own view on death. It was, as St Paul had said, 'The last enemy'.

Even so, no matter how much she loved life, as the months went by and turned into four more years, Catherine was aware that her earthly body was growing more frail. Though still mentally bright and physically fit for her years, she knew 'the last enemy' was fast approaching.

Her one personal regret was being inactive. On fine

days she loved to sit outside, gazing at the gardens and beyond to the bluebell wood. Recalling the many happy hours she'd spent tending the gardens she wondered if she would be given that job in the next world. 'But perhaps not because I don't suppose they have weeds in heaven,' she sighed.

With the rest of the family now dead, responsibility for all the family papers and letters was left with the three surviving daughters. And, just as did The Salvation Army, Catherine believed those documents really belonged, not to the Booth family, but to the world.

After reaching this decision arrangements were made for a representative from the British Library to go to North Court where the documents would be formally handed over.

There, on a July day in 1987, surrounded by walls covered with pictures in a room filled with potted plants and innumerable memories, Sarah Tayeck, the Director of Special Collections, was received by Catherine, Olive and Dora Booth.

Seated in her armchair, snugly wrapped in a plaid rug and flanked by her two sisters, Catherine proudly passed over their precious family history for the benefit of future generations.

Now, at last, she had done all she 'ought'.

Well, as at the time of her retirement, perhaps *not quite*. There was just one more obligation Catherine felt she 'ought' to fulfil. In order not to trouble other people when the time came, she went ahead and made arrangements for her own funeral, which was to be a quiet, family occasion at Finchamstead.

But being their eldest granddaughter of William Booth, founder of The Salvation Army, Catherine realised her funeral *service* would inevitably be very public and so she ordered that, 'It must take place in the evening so as not to inconvenience any of the mourners.'

On Saturday, October 4th, 1987, at her home, North Court, Finchamstead, Berkshire – just seven weeks after her one- hundred-and-fourth birthday – Commissioner Catherine Bramwell Booth was 'Promoted to Glory'.

Among the many condolences received was one from her Majesty the Queen. As on the occasion of her dedication, all the national newspapers ran reports along with the radio and television.

Traffic was halted in London's West End as nearly 1,000 people attended her funeral service at Regent Hall – the same venue as on the occasion of her one-hundredth birthday. As on that occasion, it, too, was held in the evening – not to avoid inconvenience to the mourners but because Catherine had wished it. Also, as on that one-hundredth-birthday celebration, there was happiness and laughter. This was no time for woe or weeping.

Although no daughters had married, the hall was filled with Booth relatives. There were generations of cousins, nieces, nephews and in-laws. There were representatives from all walks of life including the media, the British parliament and parliaments all over the world.

With hands clapping, the congregation sang joyfully, 'There Is A Better Land' and 'My Home Is In Heaven'. Dora, the youngest surviving member of Bramwell's and Florence's loving family, in a tribute to her sister, invited them to sing one of her favourite songs 'Tis Better On Before', adding, 'and let it rip at the rink'.

A peal of laughter rang throughout the building. But there was no disrespect in that laughter. It was simply another fusillade fired against Satan who had lost yet another soul.

Of Commissioner Catherine Bramwell Booth there could be no finer tribute than the words of her youngest sister, Senior Major Dora Booth on that day when she said, 'She was the most unselfish person. You could write across her life "Others" '.

79

And Catherine's own words on that television appearance a few years before her death are undoubtedly those she would most want to be remembered by, 'God be with you. And He will be, whether you want Him to or not'.